EXCHANGE & MART

GUIDE TO

BUYING YOUR
SECONDHAND CAR

D1827030

GUIDE TO

BUYING YOUR
SECONDHAND
CAR

JOSS JOSELYN

JAVELIN BOOKS
POOLE · DORSET

First published in the UK 1985 by Javelin Books,
Link House, West Street, Poole, Dorset BH15 1LL

Copyright © 1985 Joss Joselyn

Distributed in the United States by
Sterling Publishing Co., Inc.,
2 Park Avenue, New York, NY 10016

British Library Cataloguing in Publication Data

Joselyn, Joss
    Exchange & Mart guide to buying your second-hand car.
    1. Used cars—Purchasing
    I. Title
    629.2'222   TL162

ISBN 0 7137 1623 1

Typeset by Poole Typesetting (Wessex) Ltd
Printed in Great Britain by Cox & Wyman, Reading

Contents

1 · Selecting The Right Model

Every car is a compromise. Ideally, if we were all wealthy enough we'd have five or six – something small and nippy to drive through London, a big comfortable saloon for that business trip to Manchester, a roomy estate for the holidays, something sporty when we're in a hurry, and something economical when the funds are a bit low. What you have to decide is which type of car performs most of the functions you require reasonably well, can be bought at a price you can afford, and can be run once you've got it without breaking the bank.

People who don't carefully plan their buying can make the most bizarre choices. Cars are emotive things and there are plenty of tales about family men setting out to buy a Fiesta and coming back with an old Jaguar instead, just because they could see themselves behind the wheel of this lovely piece of prestige machinery. Another calamity was the nineteen-year-old who borrowed the money from his father to buy a Cavalier, and came back with a mileagy 3500SE Rover, only to discover it was rated Group 8 and no insurance company wanted to touch it in the hands of anyone under 25! Then there was the man who came home with a Peugeot Family estate and found it wouldn't go into his drive, let alone his garage. All those are exaggeratedly silly mistakes, but there

The Ford Fiesta is typical of the modern small, economical, versatile hatchback car.

are plenty of more minor clangers that can be dropped.

It's not a bad idea to ask yourself first why you're changing your car at all. Have your family circumstances changed? Do you need to carry more people, or less? Is the car you've got costing too much in petrol? Have you become bored with its sluggish performance and decided you want some fun with your driving? Whatever your motive, make sure it keeps a high priority and don't lose sight of it when faced with the vast number of choices available.

Much will depend on how many people you plan to carry. Most cars these days will carry four or five, but some do it in a lot more comfort than others. If there are always going to be four or five people, you want something medium-to-large. If you are only two, a small hatchback might be best. Who is going to travel in the back? If it's an ageing parent, access to the rear seat is important and you don't want a two-door model. If the rear seat is to be the children's domain, the lack of doors to open could be an advantage. If you're the type that takes everything but the kitchen sink on weekend picnics, you'll need a lot of luggage-carrying capacity. What is not wise, however, is to select your car to cope with a maximum load that occurs only once a year on the family holiday. A big car with an enormous boot and a big engine to ferry a full load around, if it's only used two weeks out of 52, is a waste. Much better to have a car suitable for 50 weeks of the year and be a little uncomfortable for two.

Similarly the idea of an estate car may be attractive; it could be handy, but is it worth the less comfortable rear seat, the increased noise, the harsher unladen ride, and possible instability in windy conditions? If it's a matter of ferrying a carrycot around, think whether a hatchback might not do as well, but if you want to carry full camping gear, then an estate could be the best buy.

The Vauxhall Cavalier range is certainly one of the most popular medium family saloons around.

Sports cars seem to have been superseded by sports saloons these days, so if this is what you want you'll have to look at slightly older models again. A true-two seater soft-top, this is the MGB.

The price of fuel has to be an important consideration, and all the time the stuff costs an arm and a leg to buy, economical consumption has an obvious attraction. Finding out a realistic average mpg figure, however, is not as easy as it might seem. The published road test figures in magazines are accurate but include a lot of high-speed testing; the mpg of the average driver is likely to be a lot better. The seller will probably display the exaggerated optimism of the archetypal fisherman, so it's not wise to accept his estimates. Probably the best bet is to take the published DOE figures and calculate an average from them. The popular method is to double the urban cycle figure, add in the constant 56 and 75 mph figures and divide by four. Even if this turns out not to be accurate on the road, it is at least a pretty good way of comparing the potential of one car against another.

Performance is a subjective matter, depending on the nature of the driver and on the sort of driving that is envisaged. A lot of long-distance open-road driving could make lively acceleration and high top speed an attractive prospect. If all the driving is to be done in congested urban traffic, high performance loses a lot of its point. If you're a steady, safe driver who regards fast car drivers as lunatics, the choice is obvious, just as obvious as it is if you're the sort of driver who could never be happy in an underpowered car! This subject is really related to the business of how many passengers you carry, and particularly so if you live in a hilly area. A heavily laden small car lumbering painfully up a long hill is a nuisance to everyone.

If you intend towing a caravan, performance must once again come into your calculations. You must have a car large enough, heavy enough, and powerful enough to cope with your proposed trailer, and if you're technically minded you'll be looking for good engine torque, rather than high BHP figures.

Most small hatchback ranges have a 'hot' version in their ranks. This is the MG Metro.

'Hot' saloons are not just restricted to the smaller cars. This is the renowned Audi Quattro.

Related to price, the specification level is another subjective matter. With everything else decided, you might still be faced with a choice between a late, low-mileage base model and an older, higher-mileage GLS or Ghia high-spec alternative for the same money. Only the buyer can decide that one.

If you're a DIY type, and these days a lot of drivers are, that's something else to think about. First, how easy is the car to service and maintain? There's not a lot that can't be tackled in the home garage on a basic Ford or Vauxhall, for instance, but a V12 Jaguar or a foreign exotic could be a nightmare. The cost of parts also has to be thought about. As a general rule, the bigger the car the more they cost, and parts for imported cars often tend to be more expensive than those assembled in Britain. Even if you have your car looked after by the local franchise garage, cost is a major factor. If they have to pay more for their parts and the car's mechanical layout means increased labour charges, it's going to be reflected in the bill. It's worth finding out, and there will be more on this subject in the next chapter.

Add to all these considerations the two mentioned at the beginning – matching the car to the garage and affording the insurance – and then you've pretty well covered the sensible side. There is, however, one more rather less practical element. Don't let all these down-to-earth matters obscure your own preferences. If you've always driven large cars and could not be happy in anything else, a compromise would not make sense; nor would it if a gutless car is a source of endless frustration, or if a petrol guzzler brings about a financial crisis every time you visit the petrol station.

The car you buy will already be a series of compromises, but if you can't compromise on your own preferences, self-indulgence is the only answer – and why not?

Here's where a buyer has to be really careful. The older a car gets the more faulty it will probably be, and although you can't expect perfection, you do need to know just what you are buying.

2 · Can You Afford To Run It?

Not many people, even when they've owned a car for years, have any idea how much it costs them to run. If asked the question, they might think vaguely about the petrol they buy, the last service bill they paid, insurance perhaps, and then hazard a guess. The odds are they would be totally wrong, most likely at least 100 per cent out!

What chance then has anyone got of assessing a car they don't yet own in terms of running costs? Surprisingly, it's not that difficult to calculate; the difficulty comes in withstanding the shock when you realise just how much any car costs.

Think for a minute that the AA's recommended rate of recompense for using a private car on company business is 26p per mile. Using the accepted average annual mileage of 10,000, that works out at £2,600 a year, or £50 a week! Those figures are based on a new car and average running cost figures, so, for a used car, the amount will tend to be somewhat less. It is possible, however, to calculate in a lot more detail than that.

For the privilege of running a car, we pay out money in two basic ways – standing charges and running costs. Let's look at the less flexible side of things first; there aren't many alternatives, when it comes to the standing charges side.

STANDING CHARGES

Depreciation

Occasionally we meet people who are able to sell their cars for more than they paid for them, but most of us are stuck with the unpleasant fact that our car is going to go down in value. In the business world, most company accountants assume a life of four years and depreciate the value by one-quarter of the cost figure annually. If you're looking for a simple method, you can do the same, but it is not very accurate. Depreciation in the first year from new, for instance, is much heavier than in subsequent years, which means on straight line depreciation it would be over-valued in the company books after one year. It also assumes that a car at the end of ten years has no value at all, when in fact it may be worth several hundred pounds.

To calculate with absolute accuracy you'd need to be able to see into the future, but you can get a reasonable idea by consulting the car price guides. If the car in which you are interested, has been around for some time, you can study the rate at which its value has dropped year by year. If you work out the percentage depreciation figure for your model, or a similar one of the same make, it is easy to apply.

The other advantage of this exercise is that you can compare the depreciation rate of one car with another. Some lose their value much more rapidly than others, and if cutting costs is your aim, those with potentially low resale value are best avoided.

Lost interest

Once you have invested your capital in a car, you are deprived of its use. You cannot now invest it and enjoy the benefits of the interest it would earn. Lost interest must be included in your calculation and, although much would depend on where it was invested, for our purposes here we can assume

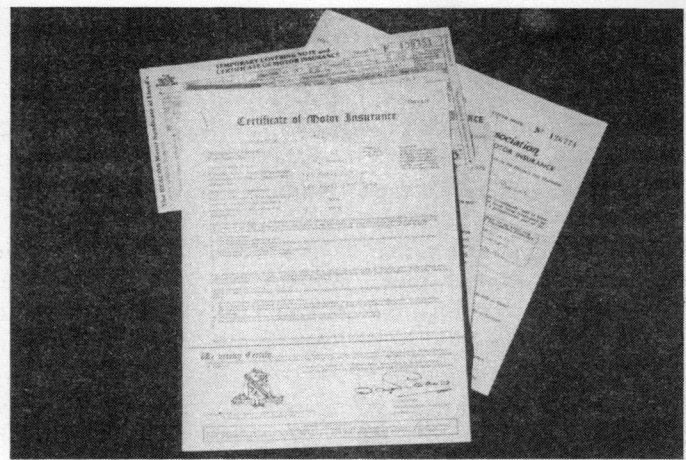

If you're 18 years old and buying a Jaguar XJS, unless you're very wealthy, think again. Insurance is something you must consider before you buy, so get a quote before parting with your money.

something like building society rate of 10 per cent. On a purchase price of £3,000, that's £300 a year, so it's worth including.

Road Fund licence

This is something the honest motorist cannot dodge. It's cheaper to buy it for the whole year as if you split it into two six-monthly chunks you pay more. You could, of course, not pay it at all, and there are a lot of motorists around who cheat in this way. If you're caught, however, the fines are enough to make the risk unacceptable, and, in any case, the yearly fee is easier to calculate.

Insurance

If you want to know if you can afford to insure the car, the easiest thing is to ring up your own company and ask what

17

they would charge. Don't stop there, though, ring up a few others as well. Premiums can be widely different between one company and another, and it's always worth shopping around. If you use a broker, he may know a company that specialises in your particular sort of risk, and that will help cut it down.

What you won't be able to do much about is the 'group' they have slotted your car into. Where it's borderline, one company might have it in a lower group than another, but insurance companies seem generally to concur. A large engine, high performance, high initial cost, luxury specification, expensive replacement parts, high body repair costs, and foreign manufacture are all factors which elevate a car into a higher insurance group.

Garaging

Just because you've got one attached to your house, it doesn't mean it's free. You pay for the privilege in additional rates, probably around one-twentieth of the total. You'll need to apply a similar proportion to your electricity bill as well, if the garage is lit by the mains supply. If you live in one of the larger towns or cities and have to park in the street, don't forget to include the cost of your Resident's Parking Permit.

Subscriptions

This item is the only one where there is any possibility of a choice. You don't have to join a motoring organisation or a club, or buy motoring magazines. If you do, however, put it down as a motoring expense.

RUNNING COSTS

Running costs is the second group of expenses and because

Fuel consumption can vary from around 50 mpg down to something like 12 mpg. The price per gallon is more likely to rise than to go down, so ensure you know what you're taking on.

they are much more flexible, they are less easy to assess accurately. We'll start with the most obvious item first.

Fuel costs

If you're using your calculations here to compare one model with another, the best way is to work out a theoretical consumption based on the published DOE figures. For second-hand cars, you cannot rely on car showroom brochures, so one of the magazines that publishes tabulated detail of used car models is the best source. DOE figures can also be obtained from HM Stationery Office. Once you have the average mpg, you will need to divide it into your annual mileage. Unless you are changing your motoring habits drastically, last year's figure will do. This will give the number of gallons, and multiplied by the current fuel cost, will give an idea of what you'll be paying.

19

Servicing

If you plan to have your car serviced by the franchised garage, the obvious thing to do is ring them up and ask what it will cost. If you're torn between several cars, make several telephone calls. The difference in costs can be enormous.

Servicing costs are vital and it is well worth investigating exactly what the regular charges are likely to be. The local franchise dealer will be able to help.

It also makes sense to get some idea of the comparative costs of parts that wear out. Tyres, exhaust, brake linings and clutch are the obvious ones. To some extent, you could do this at your local accessory shop, where they may stock the parts for all the cars you are interested in. If you're planning to do your own servicing, this is a particularly good way of assessing comparative costs, but if servicing is to be done professionally, check the prices at the franchise dealer's spares counter. Tyres and exhaust costs are best compared at one of the specialist 'instant fitting' centres.

WHAT IT COSTS

Depreciation per annum	400
Lost interest (10 per cent on £2,220)	222
Road Fund Licence	100
Comprehensive insurance (with NCD)	180
Garaging rates (1/20th of £600)	30
Garaging electricity (1/20th of £400)	20
AA subscription (basic, associate and Relay)	39
	991
Fuel (10,000 miles; 32 mpg; £2.00 per gallon)	625
Servicing	75
Replacement parts (notional)	80
	£1771

NB: £1,771 per annum is just over £34 per week.
It can also be expressed as 17.71 pence per mile.

To see how all these expenses look, we have assumed a notional four-year-old 1.6-litre car, costing £2,220. With a fuel consumption of 32 mpg and a yearly mileage of 10,000, fairly cheap to service and a notional parts replacement figure of £80, the car is reasonably average. As can be seen six out of the nine items are variable, depending on the car purchased, so it is possible to achieve figures wildly different from this, depending on what you buy.

If you've never really thought how much it costs to run a car, £1,771 per annum, or £34 per week, might surprise you, but it is by no means untypical. Fill in your own figures for the car you're going to buy and your own circumstances, and you'll be able to compare one prospect with another with reasonable accuracy.

Any of the figures can be expressed as cost-per-mile, and obviously the more miles you go the higher the cost totals are, but the lower the cost-per-mile is.

The most important thing is to be cost-conscious, to know what the car you are thinking of buying is going to cost you in hard cash, and balance this against your own and your family's needs. With these sort of figures tucked away at the back of your mind, or better still set out in a notebook, you'll be better armed when making that all-important decision about which car to buy.

3 · Buying From A Dealer

In the vast majority of British shops, if you tried to haggle over the price of goods they'd look at you in blank amazement. In the Far East or in Africa, however, they'd look askance if you *didn't* try to buy cheaper, and the shop-keepers there seem to really enjoy a good bargaining session. British car dealers are less eager to haggle, but, make no mistake, they are quite prepared to do so, and you as the customer can save quite a lot of money.

Lesson No. 1 then is not to go into a showroom and write a cheque for the figure displayed on the windscreen. That price may well have been inflated to give the salesman manoeuvring room to deal with a customer who wants to part-exchange his old car. If you're prepared to pay cash (or buy on finance), they'll usually knock a sizeable chunk off right away.

Not every dealership jacks up the price, and some actually fix the figure at the minimum the market will allow in order to bring the bargain-hunting customers in. These probably won't budge, but how do you know if the price is inflated or not? The only way is to be au fait with current prices and that means research through the latest price guides, through the local newspapers and *Exchange & Mart* to find out about the current asking value. You'll note we're still not talking about what you might have to pay; just what the 'going figure' in advertisements is.

When you ask the salesman how much he's prepared to reduce the price for a straight cash deal, he will almost certainly reach for his copy of *Glass's Guide*. It implies he's never even thought of selling for less, and gives the customer the impression he's working it out expressly for his benefit. In fact he knows to the nearest pound what he'll take for the car, and he'll use *Glass's Guide* to back up his bargaining. Known as the 'Trade Bible', it is not available to the general public and so a dealer will often use it to baffle a potential customer with science. It's worth remembering that the figures all apply to a car that is essentially in good condition and with a specified mileage, that is 12,000 miles for each of the first three years and 8,000 per annum thereafter. You should expect cars with mileages above or below this level to have

If there are more people to please than just yourself, it's not a bad idea to take the family along. The days of the 'flash' fast-talking dealer are largely over, but, on your own, you might talk yourself into something you'll later regret!

their value modified accordingly. As a rule of thumb calculation, knock off £25 for every thousand miles above the Glass's norm, and vice versa.

Although the motor trade, in some areas, does not have a very savoury reputation, don't think that every car salesman is a crook; far from it. Many work on the philosophy that a satisfied customer will come back again for his next car, and his next, and with this in mind they tidy up and respray bodywork, repair and replace seats and interior trim, thoroughly service the car and sort it out mechanically; then they offer a warranty. If you buy a car that's up to that standard, perhaps you should expect to pay a little more!

Warranties have become immensely popular in recent years and they are much better value now than they used to be. Typically, a dealer will have an arrangement with one of the specialist warranty companies and offer his range of cars with warranty already included in the price. The dealer is obliged by law to give a basic warranty of his own, but it is generally worth while to purchase one of the private extra warranties if it is not already included. If you're buying from a franchised dealership, you will probably be offered the manufacturer's warranty scheme, although this is almost certain to be insurance-company-linked and very little different from similar schemes which the warranty firm would sell under its own name.

When you buy a car that is backed by a warranty, you will find that the warranty does not normally operate for the first month. This will be covered by the dealer who sold you the car, and the idea is to prevent him selling cars he knows to be faulty and using the warranty to pay for the repairs.

The cost of the warranty will be included in the price you pay for the car, so it's something you're buying and is worth checking. Read all the small print to find out exactly what you are getting and what the restrictions are. Generally, the older the car, the more the cover will cost. You may find there are limits on the maximum amount claimable, either for parts, for labour, or both. Some schemes cover only some named parts, some limit the age of the car they will cover and others specify a maximum mileage. Make a particular point of reading up the exclusions. They will deliberately exempt anything resulting from fair wear and tear or from neglect, like a cracked head because there was no anti-freeze, or engine seizure through running out of oil. Those are logical, but there may be others you'd like to know about in advance. Certainly, also, they will insist on meticulous by-the-book franchise servicing.

It's not a bad scheme to compare the dealer's warranty with a 'private' one that you as a customer can buy direct instead of through a dealer. If you don't think much of the scheme on offer, the dealer may be able to offer something better; some schemes have a more expensive 'super' version that you can buy. Compare the benefits and restrictions and what extra benefits might be involved, like car hire if yours is off the road, recovery services after a breakdown, and even hotel charges.

The warranty you get (both the dealer's own legal obligation and the purchased warranty) are one advantage of buying through the motor trade, but there are others. Consumer protection should not be undervalued. Any car sold by a dealer must be of 'merchantable quality', which means it must be fit for its purpose. Also it must be road-worthy; it's an offence to sell a vehicle that isn't, although that applies to private sellers as well as dealers. Buying through a dealer you also get full protection from the Trade Descriptions Act and the Sale of Goods Act, and there is more about those in Chapter 9.

Buying through a large and respectable dealership is about the safest way to purchase a used car, taking advantage of all

The car's odometer is normally a good guide to how much use it's had, but after several owners remember the speedo could have been changed (or altered) and no one can really guarantee its accuracy.

the consumer protection going and getting a good comprehensive warranty, but it is comparatively expensive. It must not be assumed that such a car is not good value for money, but you certainly have to pay for what you get.

Financially, too, you might not do so well when a part-exchange deal is involved. If you are going to buy a used car, presumably the car you want to part-exchange is a somewhat older used car. The big plushy dealership certainly would not want to retail it, and the salesman when he is negotiating will know almost exactly what he'll get for it when he trades it out; compared with the going retail value, it won't be much. Now he has a choice, he can over-value the part-exchange to humour the owner and insist on getting top price for the showroom sale, or he can offer what he knows he'll get for the part exchange, and then knock something off the price of the car he's selling. He can add it on one and reduce it on the other, but if the buyer is on the ball, he won't be allowed to have it both ways. If the buyer doesn't know the value of his old car and of the one he's buying, and if the dealer is an opportunist, he can certainly lose out.

If the car he's part-exchanging is a popular model, low-mileage, in good condition and the right make, it might make good retail stock, and then the dealer will be a little more keen to do business and perhaps narrow the gap a little.

It's a good thing to remember that the important figure is not what you get on your part-exchange car, and not what you pay for the one you're buying; it's the difference between the two, the amount you actually have to pay out in order to change your car. If you get that figure worked out right before you start, it doesn't matter much how the deal is arranged.

The only way you can cut down that all-important differential figure is to sell your old car privately, or perhaps, if you're lucky, get a good price for it at auction (more anyway than a dealer might offer) and then go and buy for cash.

So much for the mechanics of 'wheeling and dealing', but there are still a couple of useful hints which are psychological more than anything else. First, never walk into a showroom totally sold on one particular car, even if your wife 'loves the colour', and your daughter's boyfriend swears it's the best car on the market. A smart salesman will spot that sort of eagerness right away, and even though he may go through all the motions, he knows he's got a sale from the moment you go in. Second, when you get to the nitty gritty, don't talk too much, not trying too hard to sell your car, and being non-committal about buying. Salesmen like things to go with a swing and you might suddenly find him making extra concessions just to fill the awkward silences, and to ensure you don't escape.

4 · *Buying Privately*

Talk to a dealer about crooks, and almost certainly he'll tell you there's no way the motor trade can compete with the general public! In fact, there's probably about the same number of villains on both sides of the fence, but never make the mistake of thinking that, because its a private sale, it has to be honest. It doesn't have to be crooked either, of course, but remember this is the area in which the buyer has least protection of all.

If you do intend buying privately, the first steps are much the same as buying any other way. You work out what sort of car you want, find out as much detail about it as you can, and form a really accurate picture of how much it should cost.

Don't just stick to the price guides, although they are a very good place to start. Carry on your price checks through local dealers' advertisements, local showrooms, etc. Check up on what the trade value of the car you're interested in is; some of the guides give trade values, or perhaps a local dealer would suggest what the value would be to him as a part exchange. All this gives you a top and bottom value, and if you're going to buy privately, depending on condition, mileage etc, you should expect to pay around half-way between the two.

Private sale advertisements appear all over the place – in local newspapers and freesheets, in specialist used car

29

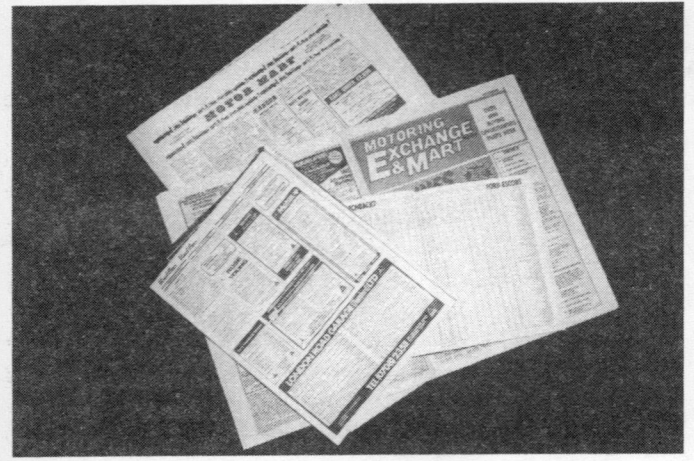

How to find out where the cars are. *Motoring Exchange & Mart* is a must, of course, but local newspapers, magazines etc all carry car ads.

marketing publications, national evening papers, and in *Exchange & Mart*. Here there are probably more sensibly priced used cars than anywhere else, and *Exchange & Mart* is also very useful for providing the buyer with excellent reference information and comparisons about current market prices. The one-time problem that the car you were interested in was being sold three hundred miles away has been largely eliminated by its division into regional issues.

Pore through as many different advertisements as you can, and although there may be a wide range, you'll be able to establish the central core of prices in which most of the cars are located. Those that are very expensive may well be wildly over-priced by people who have no idea of used car values; they might also be responsible for the lower priced ones, but it's more likely they will be cars that have something wrong, or perhaps have been put in by people who, for one reason or another, have to have a quick sale.

Now you should have a pretty good idea of what you're likely to have to pay for the car you want and can start combing the ads in earnest. In a way, they are a bit like house agents' ads – if something isn't mentioned, the probability is that it hasn't got it, but this sort of thing is best checked during the initial telephone call, along with anything else you're doubtful about. Ask about anything that isn't specifically mentioned – colour, condition, MOT certificate, model details, mileage, etc, but don't be totally misled by what *is* in the ad either. A great many car ad clichés can often be very cynically interpreted. 'Needs some attention', for instance, could mean it's a virtual wreck. 'Low recorded mileage' – a figure the seller won't guarantee. 'Mechanically sound' – bodywork's a mess. 'Recently overhauled' – a cheap rebuild that didn't work! Checking on some of those on the telephone might also save a wasted journey.

Understanding some of the advertisement detail can be a bit of a problem sometimes. To save money the advertiser may use a lot of abbreviations, and you just have to learn that RWW and HWW are rear wash/wipe and headlamp wash/wipe, that SR is sunshine roof, O/D is overdrive, LW is laminated windscreen, and T & T is taxed and MOT tested. The one that foxed me for a long time was used by people looking for a swap who would say 'exchange for a Ford Escort, BL Maestro or why'. It means 'what have you', I eventually discovered!

Look also, particularly in *Exchange & Mart,* for the letter T in brackets. This may mean that the seller is a professional trader. Even when not identified, look to see if the same telephone number recurs. If it does, it's probably a trade advertisement. Dealers do still pose illegally as private sellers, so look out for the man with a lot of cars to sell or a pocket full of log books!

Having sorted out the cars interesting enough to see, it's worth thinking about the legal aspects. These are dealt with more fully in Chapter 9, but briefly, when buying privately, the Trade Descriptions Act does not apply, and nor does most of the Sale of Goods Act. Only if the car has been wrongly described do you have any redress in law, and you would have to sue for Misrepresentation. Even this is not simple. There are three types – fraudulent, negligent and innocent, which mean more or less what they say. If you can prove the first, you could get your money back, plus damages, but in either of the second two, you can only get damages, and maybe not very much at that. The problem is that, in order to get anything at all, you have to get a solicitor and go to court. If you lose the case, you pay, and whether it's worthwhile is often debatable.

The only other possibility is that you could sue if the car was subsequently found to be unroadworthy. Selling a car in this condition is an offence, but then so is driving it (even unknowingly) so there are more problems.

All of this makes the mechanical inspection and general assessment of the car on offer even more important, and it is worth reading the chapter on this subject with particular care. Take someone with you if you can (two heads are better than one) and make sure that you look at and try everything.

Don't be put off by anything the seller says or does. Get the car out of the garage and into the open to inspect it; if you can't get it away from the garage wall, you'll not see any rust low down or be able to sight along the panels for repaired damage. Don't listen to excuses either. If it turns over sluggishly, don't believe it if he tells you he left the lights on, assume the battery is on the way out; if there's long travel on the brakes, assume the linings are worn; and if the engine runs on, assume wear, not a rich mixture, whatever the owner tells you. If he's interested in selling, he should have sorted

Remember when you buy privately that your rights in law are a lot less. Take someone with you who knows about cars and check everything just about as thoroughly as you can.

the car out before anyone came to see it.

When it comes to the time for a test drive, don't just accept it if he tells you you're not insured. He should have 'any driver' insurance if he wants to sell the car, and if he hasn't should be willing to give permission for you to drive on your own insurance. If you want to know about the car, there's no substitute for handling it yourself. Sitting beside the owner while he drives is better than nothing, but it's better to insist on driving it yourself, or even turning the car down out of hand if you can't.

Ask the owner whether he'd mind you getting an engineer's report. This is a professional assessment of the car's mechanical condition by an expert. Engineers from the AA or the RAC prepare these as a service for their members and there are other private outside firms, probably listed in *Yellow Pages,* that offer the same service. It's quite an expensive exercise, but when you consider the amount of money you can save, can be well worth while. There are snags, of course, and the chief of these inevitably is time. If the car you're after is a popular model and fairly priced, there may well be a queue of people after it. The seller will obviously let the car go to the first person offering a firm commitment and paying the money. He won't want to wait a week until the appointment has been fixed and the report produced, particularly as, in the end, it could be unfavourable. In a case like this, if you want the car, you'd probably have to rely on your own or a friend's judgement.

Bearing in mind the cost of the report, it is still best to do your own assessment first, if only to weed out the obvious rejects. You don't have to have too many duff cars looked at and rejected for the whole exercise to become uneconomic.

Even if you don't really contemplate actually having an inspection done, it might be worth asking the seller the question. A categoric refusal is a good indication that he's hiding something. If he says OK, but doesn't want to wait, you're no further forward, but there's always the thought that he just might start remembering a few faults he'd forgotten.

If you do get a professional report, it will be very thorough, so thorough in fact that you could be horrified and turn the car down out of hand. There is an art to reading one of these. The engineer will have mentioned literally everything and you'll have to assess for yourself whether you still want the car if it's borderline. Don't forget too that you can always use the evidence of the report to get the price reduced.

At this stage, before agreeing to buy, it's a good idea to ask to see the Vehicle Registration Document, which used to be called the Log Book. This doesn't actually constitute proof of ownership, but it does help, telling you who the current owner is, how long he has been the owner, and who owned the car previously. Similarly, an in-date MOT certificate doesn't give you any guarantees either, but it's some sort of indication that there's nothing disastrously wrong with brakes, steering etc and that someone has checked that the chassis isn't rusty, for instance. As a final check, get the seller to confirm in writing that (a) he owns the car, (b) there are no hire purchase payments outstanding on it, and (c) the mileage is correct. One result of this is that it confirms that you bought the car in good faith, and it will prevent a hire purchase company being able to reclaim it from you if it subsequently emerges that payments are outstanding.

As a last thought on the subject of documentation, have a look to see if the car's service records are up to date. On a much older car, particularly if there have been several owners, this probably would not apply, but for a car under say two years old, a service book with all the stamps in place and mileages confirmed can be very reassuring.

One very helpful bit of information, whether you're buying from a dealer, privately or at auction is the Service Record. Stamped and up to date it does tell you the car's been looked after.

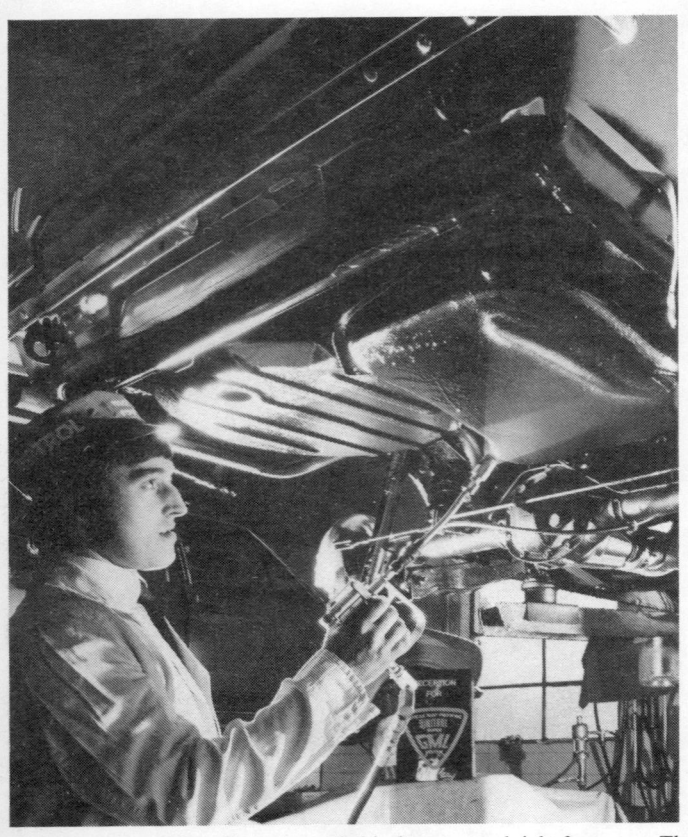

Some cars are additionally rust-proofed and guaranteed right from new. The guarantee can be a help in deciding which car to buy, but you should not expect to pay a lot extra for it.

Once you agree to buy, payment must follow the lines of normal practice and common sense. If you're going to pay by cheque, get a receipt for the money and be prepared to wait a week or so for it to be cleared. If you are in a hurry, or if the seller is in a hurry, it is possible at most banks to have the clearance 'expressed' and that could shorten the wait.

If you set out to buy and want to be able to drive your purchase away, you can obviously take cash with you, and again be doubly sure to get a receipt. Alternatives are a Banker's Draft made out to the seller, but obviously you would have to know in advance who you are buying from and the purchase price. A similar arrangement can be made to have a Building Society write the cheque to the seller and normally this would be acceptable also.

Before you get to the stage of writing the cheque, always haggle about the price. How successful you'll be will come down to a comparison between your personality and the seller's, but it is normal for him to advertise his car at a figure above what he expects to get for it. It is also just as normal for the buyer to find everything wrong that he can and offer less than the asking price. As part of this, note how much Road Tax is left. If there's a lot and the seller's forgotten it, that could be a bonus.

Finally, once you've bought the car, make sure you take the Vehicle Registration Certificate and MOT certificate with you. Then ensure you tear off the bottom section of the Registration document for the previous owner to fill in, and that you complete the 'Notification of Changes' section on the back, sign it and send it to DVLC, Swansea.

5 · *Buying at Auction*

The popular concept of car auctions is one of fast-talking auctioneers and quick-thinking, big-spending dealers. In fact, it's the place where nearly all branches of the motor trade meet and buy and sell through the auction to each other. If you remember both definitions, you won't be far wrong.

What is wrong is the popular misconception that it's a place to buy old bangers at knock-down prices. There are still a few of those around, but a high percentage of cars auctioned these days are clean, low-mileage, high class machinery, a fair proportion of it in the luxury class. In fact, at a big busy auction, you'll see the whole spectrum of cars on offer and they are being sold at the rate of about one every ninety seconds.

If you find that a bit disturbing – good! It's the first warning that, if you want to go to a public auction and buy at trade prices, on even terms with experts, then you need to know what you are doing. More specifically, you must know about cars and you must understand about the auction.

It's not a place where you can casually drop in, wave your programme negligently at the auctioneer, and drive away in a superbly cheap bargain motor car. You could buy a car as casually as that, but no dealer ever would. Buying and selling cars is their business and however relaxed they seem to be, it's all carefully thought out and planned.

That's the way you must buy too, but you cannot acquire a lifetime's experience in a few minutes, and will have to work a little differently. Decide what sort of car you want before you even look at an auction. More than that, by studying the advertisements in *Exchange & Mart* and your local newspapers, find out what the going prices are. Check those against the price guides, and read everything you can about the cars that interest you, particularly model changes. Registration dates are not an infallible guide, because you can get an older model, left behind when the new cars arrived, but eventually sold with a later registration. It does happen the other way round too, when 'next year's models' are actually in the showroom the last couple of months of the previous year and, in effect, you may be looking at a car a year younger than its registration date.

Once you know something about the models that interest you, and how much you should have to pay for them, then you can visit your first auction, but not to buy, yet. Use it as a dummy run. Look at all the cars, decide which ones you think might suit you, go into the auction hall and watch them sold. You'll be able to watch the bidding techniques and the actual procedure of the auction, perhaps identify a few dealers (they don't all wear sheepskin coats, trilby hats and big gold medallions!), and you'll also get an idea of what the auction prices are likely to be for the car you want to buy. On the walls, and probably on giveaway leaflets, you will find the auction's *Conditions of Entry and Sale,* and it's worth studying them.

When you go back to start looking for a car in earnest, you'll know a little about the auctions, but you also need to know about the cars, not just models and prices, but mechanical condition as well. You won't get a chance to drive any of the vehicles before the auction or even to hear the engine run, so you have to learn everything you can from an inspection. If you don't feel confident about doing this, take someone with you who does know cars; in any case two heads are always better than one.

You'll be looking around the bodywork for rust and for signs of accident damage or repairs and respray work. Look at the carpets, the seats and the headlining for any splits, tears and cigarette burns, and look also at the condition of the tyres. Some of these items need not put you off buying the car, but could make a difference to the price you should pay for it.

All these things you should check on any car that interests you at auction, but the best bet for the private buyer is to bid for something that's warranted. This means that the auctioneer will describe the car's mechanical condition from the rostrum before the bidding begins. If there's nothing really wrong with it, it will be something like, 'All good', or 'No major faults'. You have to listen carefully, however, because if he, for instance, specifically says, 'Some axle wear,' or 'The brakes pull to the left', those are faults you are stuck with when you buy.

If you go to one of the regular sales run by one of the major firms, like British Car Auctions, you may find an 'Engineer's Report' stuck on the windscreen, describing various aspects of the car's mechanical condition. This means that one of the auction's own engineers has driven the car and prepared the report, and this is used as the basic description for selling the car, rather than a brief description based on what the vendor wrote on his entry form. It is a lot more informative and, for the private buyer, a great boost to his confidence.

What the warranty means is that, if you buy the car and there is something wrong with it that doesn't tally with the auction's description, either from the rostrum or the

If you know what you're doing, buying at auction is not at all a dodgy business. Many of the cars are very good value for money, but remember auction terms are usually 'cash only'.

engineer's report, you can return the car. What you must do, however, is drive it immediately after you've bought it, because, in the case of a BCA auction, for instance, you've only got until one hour after the sale finishes to declare your dissatisfaction. If you do find something wrong, say, for instance, the description of the car was 'No major faults', and you discover it jumps out of gear, you draw this to the attention of one the auction's engineers. He will then either give you your money back or negotiate with the vendor on your behalf to have the price reduced. The choice of which course of action is with you, the buyer. If you fancy a car that is 'Without warranty and without reserve', be very careful. If yours is the final bid, the car is yours, whatever is subsequently found wrong with it, and you will have to pay the selling price.

Back now to before the sale begins. List the cars that interest you, carefully noting the lot numbers. Work out exactly how much you are prepared to pay for each of them. Write down a figure and stick to it.

Inside the auction hall, you can bid from almost anywhere, but, as you won't be known to the auctioneer, it's best to position yourself so he can clearly see you. What is also a good idea is to watch as the lot number you're interested in approaches. You could move briefly to where the car is parked as the auction staff climb into it, start it up and drive it into line. At least that way you can hear it start and listen to the engine.

Don't be too worried if initially the auctioneer doesn't acknowledge you and runs the price up with two others. If you've positioned yourself prominently and made your bid firmly, he probably knows you are there but he will only accept bids from two people at a time. When one drops out, he'll pick up someone else, probably you. You may not be able to see who else is bidding; don't worry about that either. If he's in the trade, he's probably got some weird personal code that only the auctioneer recognises. Just be definite about your own bidding, and be just as definite about stopping bidding. The auctioneer likes to have things clear cut. The important thing is not to be tempted to bid more than the figure you decided earlier was your maximum. It doesn't matter if you lose car after car; there's always another sale next week. More important still, don't be tempted on impulse to bid for something else because it looks good and sounds cheap. If the trade aren't interested in paying a good price, there's probably something wrong with it!

If your bid is the last and the car is knocked down to you, you will have to go to the rostrum and pay your deposit (usually 10 per cent) in cash and they will record your name and address. You won't be able to take the car or collect the log book until the balance has been paid, either by cash or banker's draft. You can pay by cheque but they will keep the car until the cheque is cleared.

At a BCA branch and some other auctions you will be asked to pay an extra sum (around £6) for non-optional indemnity. This is for your protection as a buyer and it covers you against four things; the car being stolen, being subject to unpaid finance, being a rebuilt insurance write-off, or having the mileage on the odometer altered.

If all this sounds difficult and dangerous, it shouldn't. Buying at auction is actually easier than any other way. Where else would you get such a choice of used cars, for instance, and the actual purchase is merely a matter of waving your hand and paying cash. The only difficult part is making sure you buy a good car and that's not much different from buying privately. In fact it's better, because, at auction, you are covered by the indemnity, even if you do have to pay for it. Best of all, you will be buying at trade price and that could mean several hundred pounds below the retail figure. Even if the car you buy is not clean, serviced and mechanically perfect, you could put a lot of things right with the money you've saved.

The three main things to remember are that you must know something about cars, you must know the auction ground rules, and never, never bid purely on impulse because the car sounds cheap.

6 · *Mechanical Assessment*

Whether you're buying your car from a dealer or from a private person, it's most important that you know exactly what is being offered. To pay top price for a car and then, later, find out it is eaten up with rust, or that the engine is on its last legs, is not only a great disappointment, it's also a financial catastrophe.

The answer, of course, is to carry out the most thorough check possible of the vehicle's condition, but that isn't always too easy. Ideally you need to get the car onto a garage hoist to see underneath, and have it around for a couple of days to find out about all the other aspects. You are far more likely to have half an hour at the most, and then need to make up your mind. The trick is not to waste any of the time available and check through the car in a strict planned sequence. If you got the AA engineers to test it out for you, this is how they would do it, but to use their services means making an appointment, and by that time the car might well be sold to someone else.

Even it you think you may lose the car, never be in too much of a hurry to agree to buy. This is the way to make a mistake. There are always plenty of others to go and see, and it's better to lose a good car than to find yourself landed with a bad one.

If you know a lot about cars and their mechanics, you may

well be able to inspect a prospective buy competently and make a decision, but if you aren't so qualified and don't feel confident, always try to take someone else along with you who does have the right knowledge. Even if you have a fair amount of practical knowhow, another pair of eyes and another opinion is always useful.

Start with an inspection of the bodywork, looking for rust, signs of damage or repairs, and respray work, and do it in daylight. If you try to do it after dark, even with a lead light, you'll miss something. On any car that is two or three years old, there is almost certainly going to be some rust, even if it is only chipped paintwork from stones thrown up from the road.

Deciding how serious it is is the main problem, and so important is this aspect that the whole of the next chapter is devoted to it.

Rust is always the first thing to look for, and around the front apron and the sills are important areas for checking.

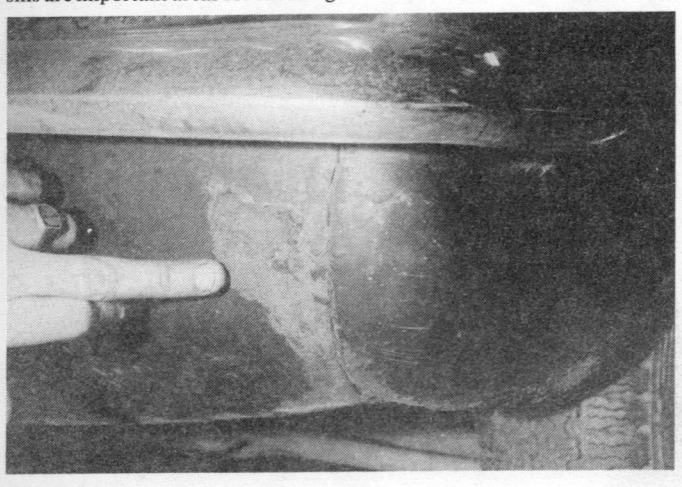

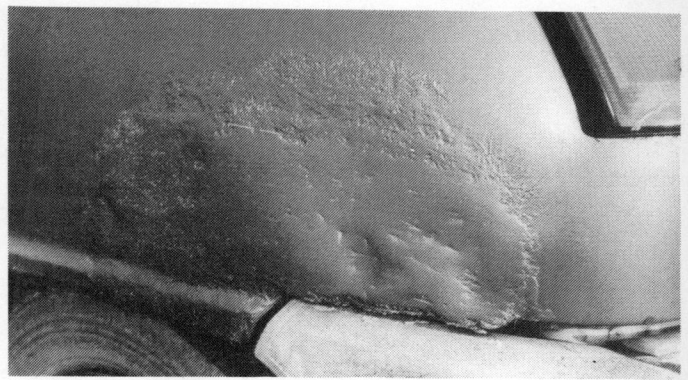

Look for signs that rust damage has been repaired in the past. You are unlikely to find anything as 'inexpert' as this, but it does suggest the sort of thing you're out to spot.

Unrepaired body damage is easy enough to see, and if you don't dismiss the car because of it, make sure that enough money has been knocked off the price to cover it. Bodywork repairs always seem to be more expensive than first anticipated.

Serious damage that has not been cleverly repaired can sometimes be seen by siting along the vehicle's sides. If you spot a rippled effect, forget that car, and go and look at something else. Slight colour differences are often a giveaway and can indicate where respraying has been done, and so can overspray onto windscreen and door rubbers, headlamp bezels and bumpers. If you do find this sort of evidence, it does no harm to ask why the work was done. If a door was dented and was repaired or replaced, have a look around the surrounds to check it wasn't more serious and that other damage has simply been filled. If one wing has been changed, carefully check the other one; rust might have been the original problem and the other wing might also be suspect.

An example here of 'under the skin' damage, and it looks as though rust is beginning to break out again. Treat with grave suspicion.

If you open the bonnet and contrast the paint colour inside with that outside, you'll possibly be able to spot if the whole car has had a respray. Dealers don't respray a car unless the bodywork is pretty tatty and it's the only way to get it presentable, so suspect the original condition and check the quality of the respray job.

Slight changes in the texture and gloss of the paint surface can indicate damage that has been filled. A small magnet is a good way to confirm this; it's only attracted to the metal and not to the plastic body filler.

Remember in all this that rust and body damage are the most difficult defects of all to cope with. You can repair or replace mechanical items a lot more easily.

Go through the car's interior with the same sort of thoroughness. Damage to seats, trims, headlining etc cannot normally be repaired, and to restore the interior's appearance the damaged item will have to be replaced. Look for wear, of course, in carpets and in seats. Damage may appear in the form of torn upholstery, cigarette burns, and gouged and scratched plastic, and if the car has had a heavy driver in the past it's possible that the seat could have virtually collapsed. Take a few deep breaths. If the car smells damp, check the carpets; if there has been a leak, you may well find the floor is rusty underneath. All these faults are disfiguring and if you don't turn the car down because of them, at least you can get something knocked off the price.

Most cars leak a little oil, but beware of anything excessive.

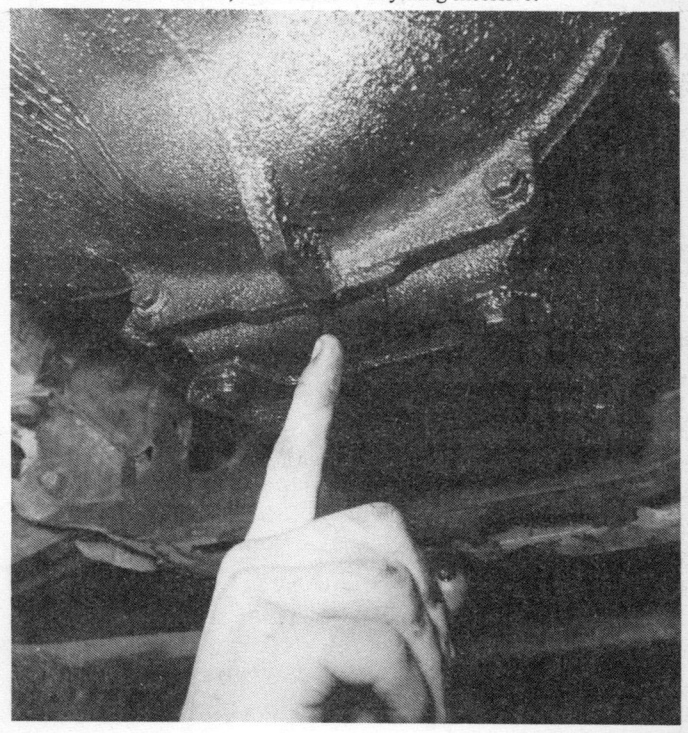

Have a look in the boot to ensure there is a spare wheel, and check the condition of its tyre. Look for the jack and wheelbrace and then have a general look round. If there is a lot of damage, it could indicate that the car has been used as a load carrier and heavily worked, particularly if it is an estate.

Look under the bonnet and as far as you can under the car. Leaks are the obvious thing you might find, particularly oil dribbling from the sump, from the clutch housing or the front timing cover. While you're peering underneath, using a good torch if you're sensible, have a look at the chassis, particularly behind the sills to see if it's rusty, and also take the opportunity to look at the tyres. They are a useful haggling point, and remember a new set could cost £150 or more.

If a general look around under the bonnet reveals a clean and cared-for engine, with all the visible levels topped up, it could indicate a careful owner. If it's too clean, however, he might be trying to hide something. Look around for water leaks, usually showing up as anti-freeze stains. An exchange radiator can be expensive enough, but carry the inspection onto the engine as well; water stains running down from the head could also be ominous.

Start the engine and listen carefully for those first few seconds. Starting from cold is when you can often pick up evidence of wear, and a nasty rattle should make you suspicious. The readiness with which the engine starts will also give an idea of the state of the battery and the starter motor.

Hopefully at this point you will be able to drive the car, but check the insurance first. If the seller is really keen to find a buyer, he should have arranged 'any driver' cover and that means you can do your testing on his policy. If he hasn't done this, suggest you drive the car on your own insurance, but remember you only get third party cover in someone else's

You should not find tyre wear or damage like this; they're both illegal. It's worth looking, however, because at very least you might find a good bargaining point.

car, even though your own may be comprehensive.

Vary your driving as much as possible. Pull away initially smoothly and gently, looking out for clutch snatch or judder and any clonks from the transmission. At some other point accelerate more fiercely; you could, in second gear and pulling hard, detect the first signs of clutch slip. Try accelerating from a low speed in third gear, with the engine labouring a little, listen for any signs of pinking or bearing

The exhaust can tell you a lot. Clouds of oily blue smoke denote a worn engine, as do oily black deposits.

knock. Try alternately accelerating hard and taking your foot off again. This will give some idea of how well a front-mounted transverse engine is braced, but if you do it in each of the gears, including reverse, you may find out whether it drops out of gear, which is an indication of gearbox wear. Perhaps the best test for this is to accelerate up a hill in second and then take your foot off suddenly.

Find a smooth camberless road and drive with your hands just clear of the steering wheel rim to see if it wanders off line at all. Then turn the car round in a restricted space, going from lock to lock in both directions. Clonking noises from a front-wheel-drive car will indicate worn driveshaft joints (knock on lock).

You will get a good idea of how well the brakes work through normal driving, but do try an emergency stop to see if the car pulls up in a straight line, and of course that they do stop the car efficiently. Check that the handbrake holds on a hill.

Stop if you can for half a minute or so with the engine ticking over, then blip the throttle hard. Watch out the back for clouds of blue smoke; a lot of it will indicate that the engine is burning oil. A look at the exhaust pipe will confirm this if it's black and oil-wet.

As much water as this is perhaps a bit of an exaggeration, but drips and trickles can mean a blown head gasket.

A shock absorber test is always worth while; more than one and a half swings means they need renewing.

Try driving over a bad bumpy surface to see how the suspension behaves. If the car 'yo-yos' badly, suspect the shock absorbers. You can check afterwards by bouncing each corner of the car in turn. Lean down heavily and release suddenly. The wing should bounce up past the level position, swing down again, and then stop. If it goes on see-sawing up

If a car looks lopsided, use a tape measure to check wheelarch height, as here. The difference could mean 'duff' displacer units on a Hydralastic suspension.

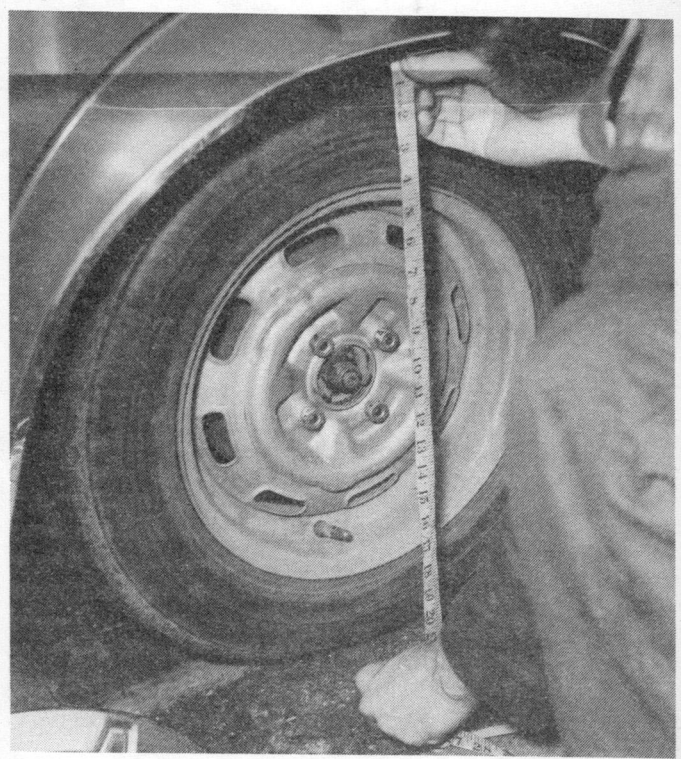

and down more than this one-and-a-half times, the shockers are worn.

With the engine good and warm, when you get back, lift the bonnet again. If there are oil fumes from the engine, it could indicate wear and oil-burning. Look a second time for leaks; with the oil hot, they will start up again, even if they have been previously cleaned away.

If you've notched up a long list of faults, you may not want the car at all. On the other hand, if you don't think they are serious, totting them all up and parading them might help you knock a lot of money off the asking price. It may still be a difficult decision to make, but at least you can make it from knowledge and not have to rely on gut-feeling and guesswork.

7 · Hunt The Rust

You can go on repairing or replacing the mechanicals of a car almost indefinitely. It's also possible to renew most of the trim and upholstery, but what usually causes a car's final last voyage to the scrapyard is the demise of the body. Rust is the killer and it is for this reason that we've given the subject a chapter to itself. When you inspect a potential used car buy, it's not a matter of deciding whether there is any rust or not; there is always rust; what you have to discover is where it is and how serious the damage it has caused.

The beginnings of corrosion are present in your car even before the manufacturer has put it together, and Mother Nature continues to try to convert every bit of ferrous metal to brown crumbling iron oxide until the vehicle is finally melted down for scrap.

The corrosion process is an electro-chemical one and requires three ingredients – water, oxygen and acid, all of which are readily available. Air contains oxygen, condensation and rain provide the water, and the acid can come from dirt and pollutants in the atmosphere, from road salts in winter or from agricultural fertilizers and farming chemicals.

It all works a bit like an electro-plating bath, and is very simple really. Remember the principle? All metals have an electrical potential and when two different ones are immersed

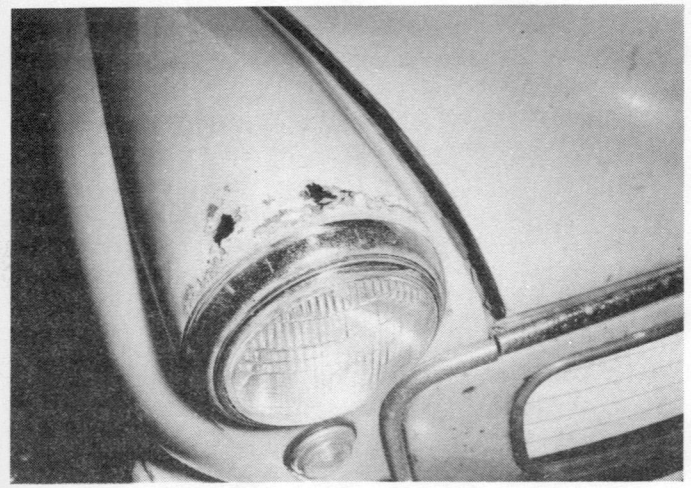

You wouldn't miss rust like this, of course, but look for more minor signs – this is how it could end up!

in an electrolyte (acidic solution), they try to even things up, with the result that metal from one is deposited on the other.

The simplest example of how it works with rust is a raindrop lying on a scratch in the car's paintwork. The bare metal under the raindrop is at one potential because it is not exposed to oxygen, while outside the drop the potential is different. If there is acid in the droplet (and our atmosphere is anything but pure), there's the electrolyte. The metal under the water is the anode and the metal outside it the cathode. When positive ions flow from anode to cathode, and negative ions from cathode to anode, rust has begun.

The obvious way to prevent rust is to cover the metal with paint and keep it covered, but in practice that is impossible. The manufacturer, with enormously elaborate rust-protection baths and modern painting techniques has in

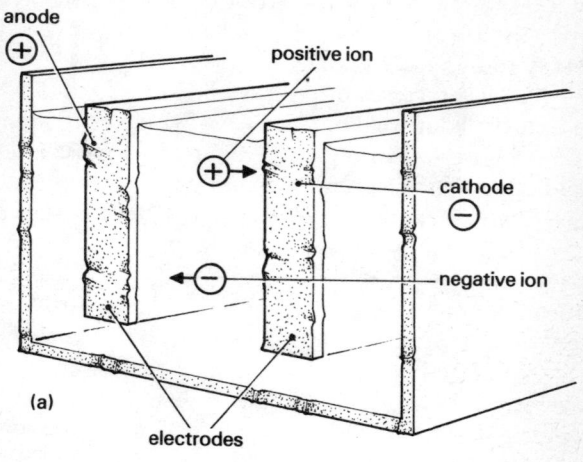

anode
⊕

positive ion

⊕→

cathode
⊖

⊖← negative ion

(a)

electrodes

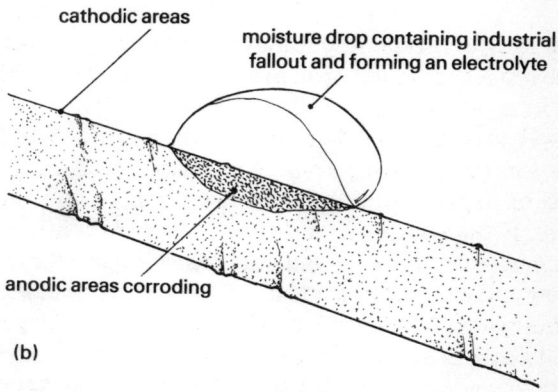

cathodic areas

moisture drop containing industrial fallout and forming an electrolyte

anodic areas corroding

(b)

This is the theory of rust; (a) how the difference in electrical potential occurs, and (b) how the electro-mechanical process works.

recent years slowed down corrosion and in some cases increased the life of his vehicles by more than 50 per cent, but the totally rust-free car is still a long way off.

The welding processes often leave tiny cracks, and when residual acids from welding fluxes are washed off, minute particles of water may not be dried out afterwards. Even if the tiny cracks are dried out, the paint covering may not fill them and subsequent flexing from engine vibration and road movement can cause the paint to crack and water to be sucked in.

Remember also that the car's underside has to withstand a constant bombardment from stones, and even the slightest paint chip back to bare metal can initiate corrosion.

Galvanic corrosion is another possibility. Go back to the initial description of the rust process which involved dissimilar metals, and you'll realise any spot where two metals are joined is a potential corrosion hazard. Even the weld metal that joins them is slightly different because its molecular structure was altered when it was heated by the welding torch. Metal fatigue has a very similar effect of changing the molecular structure, again causing galvanic corrosion.

The practical message from all this for the person looking around a used car for rust is to tell them the sort of places to look. Mud traps are perhaps the worst potential spot, where muck from the road wedges underneath, perpetually being soaked and re-soaked with acid-contaminated water, to form a perfect soggy electrolyte. There's plenty of oxygen, so rust is almost inevitable.

Metal surfaces exposed to stone damage from the road are vulnerable, and so is any metal panel liable to be damaged any other way – door edges, around locks, roof gutters and petrol filler hatches are good examples.

Any spot where there are two different metals is a potential

This is a typical mud trap. Once deposited it stays put and is repeatedly activated by rain.

rust hazard. In modern cars most decorative trims and badges are stuck in place and sealed. On older cars they were riveted, which meant holes through the body, a different metal in the rivet a potential water trap behind the trim, no wonder they rusted badly.

In doors, the cause is slightly different. Water is always likely to filter down through the seal where the window glass moves in the top of the door. At the bottom, holes are drilled to let it out again, but if they get blocked water collects, and rust starts.

One of the biggest problems is that, because rust very often starts from the underside, there may be very little evidence visible on the shiny paintwork. Because of this, it is wise to regard *any* signs of rust with deep suspicion. A line of bubbles on the paint may not look very serious, but usually, if rust is beginning to appear on the surface, it means there are holes

This tailgate rust damage is hardly typical, but it does provide an indication of what might happen if water is trapped without being detected.

Decorative trims certainly look nice, but they can often be the starting-up point for rust damage, which spreads like this from the securing rivets.

Another area where rust can start up and spread. Push back a rubber if you can to see what's going on underneath.

right through the metal. The way to find out is poke it with something sharp to see if it goes right through, but you can't do that, of course, to someone else's car you're thinking of buying. You'll just have to guess at how serious it is, although if the bubbles are immediately above a rust trap below (the top of a wing for instance) you can be pretty sure there are holes in the metal.

Perhaps if you're buying under two or three years old, you can afford to be fussy and reject any signs of rust. If, however, it's a runabout for a young driver, a housewife's shopping car, or something similar, and the price you're going to pay is very much a budget figure, then some sort of rust is inevitable. Here you are very much concerned whether the rust merely looks nasty, or whether it is dangerous and could result in an MOT failure and expensive repairs. The decision as to whether repair work is an economic possibility

Again not the sort of rust anyone would miss but it's a good guide. Note rust on an old car and look in the same place for the first signs on a newer one.

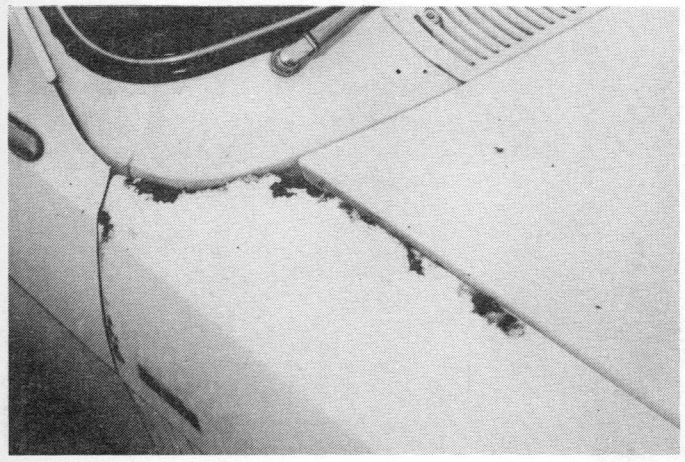

64

A nice new wing, so there's nothing to worry about, or is there? Look to see if the other one's going, and around the rest of the car.

also adds another dimension and it wouldn't be the first time someone has spent more money on putting rust damage right than the car cost in the first place.

The questions of safety and passing the MOT are linked, and if you adopt the MOT inspection criteria when checking rust, you should be able to avoid buying anything potentially hazardous. That's why a current MOT certificate is some sort of indication of soundness, but certainly not a foolproof guarantee.

Unfortunately, because cars are not all built along the same lines, it is not a simple matter for the layman to identify dangerous rust. Even when the MOT inspector is doing it, it often comes down to personal judgement, which is why sometimes a car will be passed at one MOT station and failed at another.

The MOT defines dangerous rust as when it interrupts the continuity of a load-bearing structure, but generally the MOT inspector will fail a car if there is significant rust in a load-bearing part of the body or within 12 inches (30 cm) of a suspension, steering or seatbelt mounting point.

Obviously, you can't go into all this when making up your mind whether to buy or not, but the one thing you don't want is a car that's going to fail its next test, so it might be useful to know, for instance, whether sills on the car you're looking at are load-bearing or not. Stop to think whether that wheel arch rust might have gone through into the inner panel, which is load-bearing. It's generally best to assume the worst and turn down a car if you're doubtful. The really nasty area is under the car, particularly on an older model which has a chassis or sub-frames. You don't stand much chance of being able to do a proper inspection, but generally speaking if it's rusty on top it'll be rusty underneath. It's always a good idea, if the carpets are loose just to lift them and have a look at the floor underneath; a rusty floor pan can bring MOT failure and can be very expensive to repair with new panels.

Once you've made up your mind what model you want, check up if you can what the most likely and expensive rust areas are. Chapter 8 gives some help here, and the sort of things you'll be checking are rear subframes in the Mini, MacPherson strut front suspension mountings on older Fords, chassis outriggers on the Triumph Herald; all the notorious weak spots in fact.

If the car you're looking at is a real giveaway bargain, it could be profitable to remember that it is possible to repair rust damage by replacing the complete damaged panels, but it is expensive, and for that reason only ever contemplate it on a car that's practically given to you. That way, if the repair estimates are totally uneconomical, you don't lose too much and the gamble was a sensible one. Similarly, a classic model with collectors' value might be a good buy, rust and all.

Purely cosmetic repair of rust is certainly possible, even as a DIY exercise, using one of the popular body filler kits, but do make sure the damage is not widespread and that it is within your capabilities, *before* you buy the car.

Also while you're buying, check that someone hasn't carried out some cosmetic rust repair work already. If it's been really well done, you won't find it easy to spot, but a DIY job can be visible as a change in the texture of the paint's shine, as a ripple or bump on the surface, or as a change in the colour. Again, the areas to check are the ones known to rust, and a good way is with a small magnet – it is not attracted to body filler!

One more aspect of rust is that you may be offered a car with an in-date warranty. Many manufacturers now have

No comment needed about this sort of repair, but even if you're only paying a few pounds for an out and out banger, remember you've still got to get it past the MOT Test.

them lasting for up to six years. Some are based on the standard vehicle as it rolls off the production line, while others are additionally treated by one of the specialist rust-proofing companies, but what in fact do they offer? First, they don't guarantee that your car will not rust; they merely guarantee to put things right if it does. Not quite that either; in many cases the rust has to specifically start underneath and work its way through the metal, so in fact what you get is a 'perforation guarantee'. Sometimes there are 'exceptions', like rust spreading from body seams, and when you remember welded joints are a noted starting point you can understand why they are not included.

Many of the warranties stipulate that the car must be inspected and re-treated a number of times during the time of the cover, and this is something that you have to pay for. If the car isn't regularly treated, the guarantee may be invalidated.

All this is not to say that rust-proofing is not worth while, nor does it mean that a warranty with a used car does not have some value, but it is worth reading the small print, seeing how long it has to run and assessing just what it has to offer, before paying out any extra money for the privilege of having it. Remember, if you buy the car, you'll get the guarantee whether you want it or not, so is it worth paying for?

8 · *Model by Model*

In this chapter are highlighted some of the more common faults on a few of the most popular used car buys. From the hundreds of different models available throughout the used car market, 22 have been selected and for each of these are signposted some of the more prevalent rust areas and some of the mechanical weak points.

It is obviously not possible to list every fault, even with a limited number of models, so these 'instant pointers' should be used in conjunction with all the other more in-depth information in the rest of the book, particularly Chapters 6 and 7.

When you make out a checklist to apply to a potential used car buy, these are the points you must include, but not the only ones. Talk to people who've owned the model, and particularly, if you can, someone who has worked on it, and you'll be able to add some more items of your own.

Forewarned is forearmed – that's what it's all about!

AUSTIN MINI

Rust has always been the biggest problem with the Mini and there are a lot of places to check, especially on an older model. Look at the seams all over the body, but particularly at the area around the front headlights. Inspect the outside corners of the front scuttle under the windscreen, wings, sills, rear boot lid, and inside the boot. On the estate versions, check the front bottom corner of the rear wheel arches inside the car. Underneath, the most important place is the rear sub-frame; if it needs a new one, you can knock a lot of money off. On estates the fuel filler neck rusts and that can mean a new tank.

The engine does not give a great deal of trouble until around 60,000–70,000 miles, but if the mileage is in that area, it might need an overhaul soon. Make sure you try the synchromesh on all the gears; changing that gearbox isn't easy. Also listen out for a worn idler gear.

Turn the steering from lock to lock. If there's a clicking

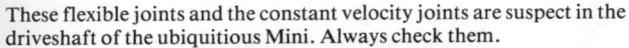

These flexible joints and the constant velocity joints are suspect in the driveshaft of the ubiquitous Mini. Always check them.

Lever arm shock absorbers are the Achilles heel on the Morris Marina. Bounce the front wings to check.

noise, it will probably mean new constant velocity joints. Look at the height of the body. If it's sagging in one corner, it might mean trouble with the cones and knuckles on a dry suspension or defective displacer on a Hydrolastic.

AUSTIN METRO

Being a very much later car (first launched in 1980, and using the well tried engine and transmission of the Mini), there are less trouble spots to look for on the Metro. Pay particular attention to the clutch, which has a tendency to judder, look for oil leaks underneath and go round the cooling system, again looking for leaks. Braking is a lot better on models fitted with a servo, and it could be worth checking around the front apron and under the rear wheel arches for stone damage and perhaps the beginnings of rust.

MORRIS MARINA

You'll need to look for rust on the older Marinas and around the headlights and tops of the wings is a good place to start. Check around all the wheel arches and pay particular attention to the sills, which are load-bearing on this car and rust would mean an MOT failure.

Front shock absorbers are a weak point and might well need changing, so the bounce test is a must. The engines are quite robust but tend to burn a little oil as they get mileagy. Clutch judder is a common fault and not always easy to cure. Look also for signs of synchro wear in the gearbox; it tends to show up initially on second and third gears.

AUSTIN PRINCESS/AMBASSADOR

Early problems of drive shaft breakage on the 2200 and general unreliability gave this model a poor reputation which was difficult to lose, even when the problems were cured. On late models there are very few specific faults. Look for rust in all the usual places, but pay particular attention to the headlamp area, not because they're vulnerable, but because they are expensive to replace. For the same reason it's worth looking at the Hydrolastic suspension system; replacing displacer units is a costly business.

Pay particular attention to the tyres. This model is sensitive to steering adjustments and tyres can wear if the geometry needs adjusting. Being front-wheel-drive, it's as well to check the drive shaft joints by driving on full lock; if they click they need replacing. A final tip – buy a model with PAS steering, as it's very heavy without it.

AUSTIN ALLEGRO

Power units for this car are borrowed from the Mini (1100

and 1300) and the Maxi (1500 and 1750). With the small engine, chatter from the idler gear is worth listening for. It's a warning, because if it breaks up you'll need a new transfer gear housing and possibly a new gearbox. On the bigger-engined models possibilities of trouble are the gearbox, the driveshafts, and wheelbearings. Noise is the clue in all three cases and all can be expensive. Top and bottom swivel joints can be a problem, not really being man enough for the job they do. Rusting is not a major fault with the Allegro, but check all the usual places anyway.

ROVER SDI

The wedge-shaped body of the SDI Rover, like any other car, is susceptible to rust. The bonnet is one place to look. The drainage system works by channelling water down the sides and out through holes at the front end. If they get blocked, water is trapped and a rusty bonnet is the result. There are more drain holes in the doors and the same trouble can arise there. Put the sills on the list and also the area under the bonnet behind the front suspension mounts.

The Rover's other Achilles heel is the smaller engine which has a nasty habit of burning out valves. It's curable, but it isn't always easy, particularly if all the shimmed valve clearances have to be sorted out from scratch. On the V8 engine it is the camshafts that are the problem, along with the rocker shafts which can wear badly if the oil isn't changed regularly.

TRIUMPH DOLOMITE

This is really a range of cars, all with the same basic body shape and the same Dolomite name but ranging in engine size. There's a 1300, 1500, 1850 and the 2.0-litre Sprint, and they were sold between 1976 and 1981. Rust was never a

You can't tell much from the outside of a smart alloy head, but where one is fitted, always double-check for coolant leaks around the head joint and for any other signs of a blown gasket.

major problem, but the places to look are along the bottom of doors, base of screen pillars, wheel arches and in the boot floor. The larger-engined cars featured an alloy head and had a history of gasket troubles, often resulting in warping. With only a 0.020 in maximum skim possible, it could mean a new head and that's expensive. Similarly using the wrong anti-freeze at some time in the past could have resulted in corroded water passages and coolant leaks.

FIAT STRADA

Fiat learnt their lesson with a few of their other models and they've really overcome rust problems now. Nevertheless, have a look at the top and bottom of the doors on early models where the seams can rust. Check the front edge of the bonnet; that's also suspect, as is the bottom of the tailgate, also since redesigned.

Inside, the seats are worth looking at. If spring that support them are broken, it means a new seat and that's expensive. Try reversing a bit sharply and taking your foot off; if the lever jumps out of gear, it's a gearbox rebuild. Finally check if the speedo is working. It's electronic and the sensor in the gearbox can fail, costing a lot of money to renew.

FORD FIESTA

Certainly not known as a 'rot box', the Fiesta nevertheless does have a few corrosion prone points. The back of the headlamps is one place to look; they have been known to rust so badly they come adrift. Door edges are worth checking, and also the hinges which can wear as well as rust. The fuel tank can be suspect, and, along with the more obvious spots like sills, it's worth looking around the filler cap. Take the spare wheel out and check the well floor which is another rust risk, and, still talking about corrosion, but of a different kind, inspect the radiator for leaks. It's not an enormous problem, but could provide a useful haggling point.

CV joint and steering rack gaiters tend to split, and if they have on the car you look at, it could mean a new rack or joints, neither of which are cheap.

FORD ESCORT (RWD)

In the rear-wheel Escort, rust was never a major problem, but obviously the older the model, the closer it needs looking at. Check particularly the front MacPherson strut mountings under the bonnet. Corrosion here is an MOT failure, and

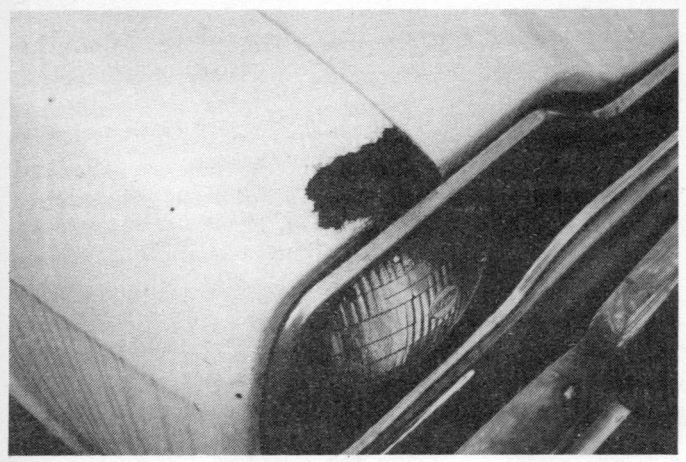

This is an Escort and the rust patch tells its own story; another Achilles heel.

although it can be repaired, it may not be cheap. Front wings may be suspect at the rear end and at the front, behind the headlamps and front apron.

Engines are usually good for around 60,000 miles before they start using oil and then it is likely to be piston and bore wear that's the trouble; look for fuming and a sticky black exhaust pipe. See if you can see an oil leak at the rear of the gearbox. It can empty it of lubricant, so if you see traces check the gearbox carefully for damage. Also have a look at the radiator for signs of leakage. It's not cheap to renew.

FORD ESCORT (FWD)

Not around long enough to give much of an indication of corrosion, the fwd Escort nevertheless should be checked out. Look at the front strut mountings, around and under headlamps, the leading edge of the bonnet, sills and floorpan. Look also at the front apron and rear-wheel arches, checking for stone damage.

Other points to investigate are the front brake discs, which can show wear at 20,000 miles, and the carburettor. The Ford VV unit can have problems with the choke and the control diaphragm.

FORD CORTINA

Unless the Cortina is being bought as a 'collector's' item, you'll probably be considering the MK IV or later, that's from 1976. Much better than the earlier MK III in its rust-

Under the bonnet of Ford Cortinas and Escorts rust can attack the top mountings of the big MacPherson strut shock absorber units. It's an MOT failure unless repaired with properly welded in new metal sections like here.

This is the overhead camshaft of a Ford Cortina. Many were sound, but some wore out camshafts in very short order. You can't see it, of course, but listen carefully to a 1600 or 2000cc Ford ohc engine on Cortina, Capri and Granada.

proofing, it still needs checking around sills, wheel arches, and door bottoms.

Ford engines are generally very good, but beware of the 1600 and 2000 OHC. Some have been known to have three new camshafts and still give trouble, in spite of new oil feeds, etc. Others never show signs of a problem, but if the top end clatters on the car you're looking at, leave it alone. The propshaft is the other item to check. It's elaborate with a number of joints and can be expensive to renew.

FORD CAPRI

Like most Fords the Capri is not particularly susceptible to rust, but early models particularly need to be checked just the same. Blocked drain holes under the doors can cause rust there, and it's well worth checking the headlamps as well. Look at wheel arches and sills, and also the front apron for stone damage. Most of all check the front strut suspension mountings under the bonnet. Rust there is an MOT failure.

Remember that some Capris, like Cortinas, have the 1600 or the 2000cc overhead cam engine. If oil changes have been neglected, failure could be imminent; listen very carefully for top end clatter. Other points to check are the gearbox for bearing wear, propshaft for UJ's on the way out, and front discs for distortion.

JAGUAR

Everything on a Jaguar is bigger and more expensive than other cars and so you'll need to be twice as careful. The engine will cost a fortune for a major overhaul, so look first at oil pressure which should be at least 40 psi with the engine hot. Check also for signs of overheating, particularly the 4.2 model. Air bubbles in the radiator or water dripping from the exhaust might just be a head gasket but suspect cracked block or head.

Bodywork is even more important on a Jaguar, which, because it's a prestige car, has to look good to sell. In the region of the headlights is one place to look for rust, also round wheel arches, doors (particularly hinges), and the boot floor. The petrol tanks can be suspect too and even the exhaust costs a small fortune to renew. The trick on these cars is to check everything, because each item you miss will hit you in the pocketbook.

The complex power house shoe-horned under the bonnet is actually on the new Jaguar AJ6, but there are two points. If you're paying anyone to work on one of these, or anything like it, you need an expert and it will cost a lot. Also, again unless you're an expert, DIY is out of the question.

NISSAN (DATSUN) CHERRY (100A)

No inherent engine problems on these cars. If they pull well, don't clatter, and there's no fuming or exhaust smoke, they're probably OK. Try listening to the gearbox for bearing whine and accelerate hard in second gear to see if the clutch slips. Make the usual check of driveshaft gaiters; splits could mean an expensive replacement.

Very early models could be rusty, so beware, but on all models check the top front suspension strut mountings for corrosion which could mean an MOT failure. Bottoms of doors, sills, rear wheel arches and front wing tops are further places to look.

NISSAN (DATSUN) SUNNY

Like the Cherry, engines are very durable on this model and mileages often go to 120,000 before a major overhaul. Make the usual checks, however, for oil burning or low oil pressure, although you can usually ignore valve gear clatter or timing chain rattle. Gearboxes are equally reliable and usually slick. If the gearchange feels wrong, don't buy the car.

Corrosion can be a bit of a problem on the Sunny. As usual, front wing tops and further inside the bonnet where the struts are mounted are two very important check points. Blocked drain holes in the bottom of doors can cause nasty rusting there; also have a look at the rear wheel arches and the rear suspension mounting points. The latter could be an MOT failure. Looks also for rusty brake pipes and badly worn suspension joints.

RENAULT 5

The R5 engine is a robust unit, quite capable of more than 100,000 miles without a major overhaul. The problem is that, when it is necessary, you can't get a short motor and a complete engine is very expensive. A good point is that even when it does wear, the valve guides are likely to be the first to go and that's just a top overhaul. If you detect timing chain wear, however, it's an 'engine out' job to change it. The head is alloy, so remember that the effects of overheating in the past might have caused warping and wrong anti-freeze might have resulted in gasket leaks; it might also have done the wet liner base seals a mischief.

Rust will first appear in the wheel arches; mud traps are responsible at the rear and restrictions due to the spare wheel housing at the front. On older models check all the box members and the floor under the car, the sills and door bottoms, and the floor inside as well. Look particularly hard at the rear end underneath where severe rust can write off the car.

TALBOT AVENGER

This is a car that's been around a long time, so rust is an important factor. Front wings can be suspect, particularly around the headlamps and right at the other end near the front door leading edges. Under the bonnet, top mountings of front strut suspension units need looking at, because rust here is an MOT failure. Check the sills, especially the inner members and up along the rear wheel arches. Door bottoms might also rust if the drain holes have been blocked.

The rest of the checking on this model follows conventional lines, but engine, gearbox and final drive are all pretty robust. Try the dampers, particularly the MacPherson struts on the front; they're expensive to renew.

TALBOT ALPINE/SOLARA

Go for the worst point first, which has to be the transmission on these cars. Two problems: firstly, because of the design, 2nd gear can give trouble after about 20,000 miles; Secondly, if the front oil seals go, the oil goes with them, the box overheats and perhaps even seizes. It's an expensive unit and if engaging second is difficult, look for another car. Check the driveshaft gaiters for splits or damage. A worn joint means a new (and expensive) shaft.

The Alpine does not have a bad reputation for rust, but there are plenty of mud traps underneath and it's worth checking. Look in all the usual places but particularly around wings, sills and rear apron.

This is the transmission unit out of a Talbot Alpine. These units have been known to have their problems, so be very careful when buying; get a wrong'un and all that lot might have to be renewed.

VAUXHALL VIVA

Like any car that's been around for a long time, there are going to be some rusty examples. To make sure you don't buy one, there are a lot of places to look. Start with the wheel arches, at the edges particularly, around the headlamps, bottom corners of the front screen and the rear of the front wings where drain holes get blocked and rust right up the door pillars. Two particular spots are the inner front wing panels (that can write off the car) and the lower rear suspension arms and their mountings.

On the mechanical side, listen out for noisy timing chain on early engines, top end noise (cam followers) on the 1800 engine, oil leaks, water leaks (radiator particularly), ball joints and propshaft.

VAUXHALL CAVALIER (RWD)

This model seems to be one of those least troubled by rust. Stone damage under the front bumper is possible and perhaps a little rust in the seams. On the more up-market GL and GLS models, water trapped behind trims could result in minor corrosion and the petrol flap too attracts it. The wheel trims deteriorate badly, and finally it's always a sensible idea to check out sills and wheels arches.

Not a lot goes wrong mechanically either, and 100,000 miles is not unknown before an engine overhaul. Camshafts can wear, but usually the noise can be ignored; the clutch tends to be heavy but that you get used to, and the harsh growl in reverse is normal too. It's worth checking on steering rack gaiters, dampers (bounce test), and the propshaft.

VOLKSWAGEN GOLF

Rust is not a serious problem, but it can appear in the wings, sills and door bottoms; displaced seals can accelerate the latter.

First signs of engine wear might show up after around 50,000 miles, but oil smoke from the exhaust is probably worn valve guides and will only involve a top overhaul. Because of the OHC configuration, a blown head gasket can be difficult and it may involve reaming camshaft bearings as well as re-skimming. The clutch wears well and any juddering is more likely to be a broken lower mounting. Noisy gearbox bearings after 50,000 miles probably won't need any action – they seem to go on for ever.

9 · *Your Rights In Law*

Ask the Office of Fair Trading what generates the most complaints from the public, and the answer will certainly be the motor car. Apart from a house, it's probably the most expensive thing that any of us buy. Unfortunately, however, unlike bricks and mortar, cars have a relatively short life, and, being mechanical, are used and abused throughout that time. Worse than that, it's not just the cars that are dodgy; the morals and motives of the people dealing in them can sometimes also leave a lot to be desired.

We always think of the innocent private buyer being taken for a ride by the unscrupulous motor dealer, but, if you talk to people in the trade, they'll have an enormous fund of tales to illustrate how dishonest the general public is. There is no such thing as a perfect used car and human nature is never at its best when involved in 'doing a deal'. It's not surprising therefore that the law has become more and more involved and much of it is concerned with protecting buyers against being ripped off, either by the trade or by their own kind. Total protection is a bit optimistic, however, and it's obviously going to be an advantage if you know just what the law can and can't do to help before you go out and buy.

BUYING FROM A DEALER

The dealer, when he sells you a car, has to meet certain conditions. Under the Trade Descriptions Act, for instance, the car must be exactly as portrayed in any advertising. If it was described as a 1982 model and you later discover it is a 1981 car, or if the mileage is different from the advertisement, he hasn't fulfilled the condition. The dealer is supposed to investigate the history of the car and in practice what he does about mileage is to get the previous owner, if he can, to sign that it is accurate. If he has any doubt at all, he probably won't guarantee the reading. The penalties for making a false declaration are severe and an honest dealer certainly wouldn't take the risk.

The law also says that the car must be of 'merchantable quality'. This is the cornerstone of the Sale of Goods Act, passed, believe it or not, before there was even a used car market at all, in 1893. There are exceptions to it, however, based on the notion that there's no such thing as a perfect used car. The exceptions are defects drawn to your attention before you bought the car, or any other defects that ought to have been quite obvious when you examined it. If the dealer told you that the radio didn't work, you can't take it back afterwards and demand he repair it. Similarly, if there was a whacking great dent when you examined it, which you must have seen, you can't demand to have that put right either. The car must be 'reasonably fit for its particular purpose' either when you have made the purpose known to the seller before buying, or where it should be patently obvious.

If the dealer does not fulfil all these conditions, you can either reject the car and get your money back in full, get some of the money back (damages), or get compensation as repair costs.

A lot will depend on the particular circumstances, but the first thing to do is notify the dealer, preferably in writing, that you want your money back. If you delay, you may lose the right to reject the car and only be able to get damages. Similarly you must not accept an offer to repair or take any money, and you should not drive the car at all. Any of these could result in you getting damages rather than your money back.

BUYING PRIVATELY

In this situation you're not in nearly such a good position. If the seller isn't in the car business, 'fitness for purpose' and 'merchantable quality' do *not* apply.

About the only way you can reject it is by proving 'misrepresentation', but that's difficult unless you get the seller to write down what he tells you and sign it, or you have a third party witness present at the time. If the car does not tally with the description in the advertisement or with details on a receipt, however, this is evidence that would stand up in court. Even then you'd have to engage a solicitor to represent you, and if you lost the case it could be expensive.

The whole subject of 'misrepresentation' is also a lot more complicated than that. There are three kinds – fraudulent, negligent and innocent. If the first is proved, and you were deliberately conned, you will be able to return the car and get your money back. 'Negligent' is when the seller wasn't aware of the misrepresentation, but should have taken more trouble to check, say, something like mileage, and here you'll only get damages.

If the seller had no reason to know the facts were wong, that is termed 'innocent' misrepresentation. Here you might still get damages, but they won't be much.

Apart from misrepresentation, the only other way you can repudiate your purchase is, in a very extreme case, to affirm that the car is virtually 'a heap of scrap' and not a car at all!

Alternatively, perhaps, you could report the seller to the police for selling a car in unroadworthy condition. That's an offence, but be careful because so is driving it!

BUYING AT AUCTION

Auction buyers have very little protection in law, particularly if they buy a vehicle 'As seen, and without warranty'. If you make the winning bid and the car is knocked down to you, you have completed a contract in law and are liable for the full amount of money.

If there is anything wrong with the car, you have no redress in law against the auctioneer. The only possibility is that of 'misrepresentation'. The car must conform in every way to the auctioneer's description of it.

The status of the vendor might be relevant. Technically, if he is selling privately, the law's obligations of 'fitness for purpose' and 'merchantable quality' do not apply. If the seller is a trader, they should, but in practice much depends on the fine print in the auction's *Conditions of Entry and Sale*.

Many auctions, recognising the legal hassle that can result from some of the more unscrupulous members of the motor trade manipulating and misusing auctions for their own purposes, include an indemnity with every car sold. It's paid for by the purchaser (he can't opt out) and indemnifies him against (a) the car being found to be stolen, (b) the car being the subject of outstanding hire purchase, (c) the warranted odometer reading subsequently proving to be false, and (d) the car having been an insurance company 'write-off' and not so declared at the auction. All this provides useful legal guarantees for the private buyer at auction, but does not, of course, compare with the sort of warranty that can be obtained when buying from a dealer.

WARRANTIES

The warranty scene is much better nowadays than it once was, and one of the major steps towards this was the 1973 Supply of Goods Act which stopped the use of exclusion clauses to deprive the buyer of his rights under common law. Now warranties are an additional reinforcement of the basic protection.

Typical warranty schemes are often insurance company backed, run for 12 months, and the cost is automatically included in the price of the car. To stop dealers unloading a rogue car and covering it at someone else's expense, the warranty term does not usually begin until a month after the sale; the first four weeks the dealer has to cover himself.

Usually the warranty is worth having, particularly if it's included in the price, but it does pay to read the small print carefully. Restrictions may include things like the components covered, price ceilings, mileages etc. There are probably conditions too, one of the most common being that the car must be regularly serviced. It's essential to make sure all the conditions are met because it won't make any difference when you finally want to claim that what you're claiming has nothing to do with servicing. If you've broken the conditions, however irrelevant, they'll refuse to pay the benefits.

Knowing your rights is one side of the coin; knowing how to invoke them is the other. Generally, if you have a problem, the best thing is to try to solve it without going to the law. Go back to the vendor first and, if it's a dealership, follow that by contacting the Motor Agents Association or the Society of Motor Manufacturers and Traders (provided he's a member) who operate a code of practice. If you want to go to law, initial advice from a solicitor is always a good idea, or if you are a member of one of the motoring organisations you are probably entitled to legal advice from them.

Perhaps the best thing of all was the establishment of the Office of Fair Trading back in 1973. Your local Trading Standards Officer has wide powers related to consumer protection and is almost certain to be able to help. Your local telephone directory should be able to supply his address.

10 · Raising The Money

If you know you're going to need to borrow money in order to buy your car, check up on the different possibilities before you go out looking at cars. Some ways can cost you twice as much as others; but the Consumer Credit Act provides a 'rule of thumb' indication of comparative cost. Now, by law, in addition to the flat rate of interest payable on a loan, the APR (annual percentage rate) figure must also be given. It's usually just about double the flat rate interest figure. The latter doesn't take into consideration that, as you pay off the loan, you are diminishing the amount you owe while continuing to make the same monthly payments. At the end of the period of the loan, therefore, you will be making very high monthly payments compared with the actual amount owing. What the APR does is to consider all this, including an arrangement fee if one is charged, put it all into perspective, and give you a figure you can compare with other similarly-computed figures. Look, therefore, for a loan arrangement where the lowest possible APR is quoted.

Details of schemes and the rates charged vary, but there is a generally accepted cost hierarchy. The methods are described below from the cheapest up to the most expensive.

Most insurance companies will provide an *insurance policy loan* against endowment or whole life policies, and sometimes they will give advances against unit-linked policies as well, but obviously they must have a high enough cash-in value. Once they've advanced the money, they will deduct it from the amount due on maturity, and all you pay is interest. The APR is likely to be in the region of 10–16 per cent, depending on the company, and as you don't have to pay back the money you've borrowed until it's deducted from the sum finally payable, your annual payments also tend to be low. Using this method you can usually borrow up to around 90 per cent of the policy's cash-in value and they probably won't even ask what the money is for. Finally, as they'll keep the policy as security, they won't need to check up on your creditworthiness.

A *bank overdraft* can be planned and pre-arranged with the bank manager and can be a reasonably cheap way of borrowing money. Theoretically, all you need is a current account and a sympathetic bank manager, but get used to the idea that he'll probably ask a few questions. He'll want to know what you want the money for and how you intend paying it back, and both the amount and the time you can borrow it will have to have his agreement. Depending on why you want the money, he may possibly suggest a loan instead. The advantage is that you pay interest only on the amount of money you are overdrawn; so that if for much of the month you're not overdrawn at all and only as you approach payday you start to pay interest, an overdraft could be very economic.

Interest rates vary depending on how good a risk you are, but generally are likely to be a few per cent more than the current bank base rate. The APR could be in the region of 14–18 per cent, but don't forget that being overdrawn means that you start paying bank charges, or pay them at a higher rate. Depending on how much you use your bank, that could be expensive.

For an *ordinary bank loan,* it's again a case of going for a chat with your bank manager. This time, however, you could borrow it for a longer period, a matter of years rather than months. The APR will probably be in the same region as an overdraft (around 14–18 per cent) and this is cheaper than a *personal bank loan,* which you can get from any of the high street banks, even if you don't bank there, provided, again, that the bank manager approves the deal. Repayment is by equal monthly instalments at a fixed rate of interest, and the instalments include the interest. The APR will be 17–19 per cent, depending on how long you take to pay it back.

A finance company personal loan is much the same as a personal loan from the bank and you can usually borrow up to about £5,000 over a period of up to five years. Like the bank loan, the interest is fixed for the whole period of the loan, but the difference is that it's likely to cost more. It may not be much more, around 21 per cent APR perhaps, but it could be up to 30 per cent.

One early snag with a *credit card buy* is likely to be the credit limit. In most cases it is under £1,000 and you may well want to pay more than that for a car. When it comes to the cost of borrowing, if you pay the whole amount within 25 days of the statement you don't pay any interest charges at all. If you only pay off the minimum amount permissible shown on the monthly statement, the APR will work out at just over 23 per cent; less if you pay if off more quickly.

One of the major differences with *hire purchase* is that the car is not yours until you've finished paying for it. You are, as far as the law is concerned, hiring it from the finance company who has bought it from the dealer. Normally, you'll be expected to pay a deposit and then pay the rest in monthly instalments over a pre-determined period; three years is typical. The APR might be anything between 20 and 40 per cent, but can be less, particularly if interest-free credit is being offered. If you are lucky enough to find someone offering cheap or interest-free credit, be particularly wary that the cost of the finance hasn't simply been added to the price of the car. If it has, you might do better to borrow the money from your bank, and find a cheaper car to buy.

As the car belongs to the finance company until you've paid the final instalment, they can repossess it any time if you don't keep up the payments, but, unless it involves a hire purchase price of more than £7,500, once you've paid one third of it the finance company will have to get a court order to repossess. If you decide you don't want the car and don't want to go on paying, you can end the agreement by giving the car back, provided your payments are up to date. Sometimes, however, you might have to make the figure up to half the HP price, and in any case you would be expected to make good or pay for any damage.

There is a vital difference between HP and a *credit sale;* with the latter you actually own the car. You can be taken to court and sued for payment, however. If you sell the car before the last payment has been made, you must pay off the loan, although not necessarily immediately.

Index